CONCEPT AND RECIPES BY **ERNST LECHTHALER**

PHOTOGRAPHY BY **AMIEL PRETSCH**

TEXT BY **AUGUST F. WINKLER**

Rum Drinks & Havanas
Cuba Classics

ABBEVILLE PRESS **PUBLISHERS**

NEW YORK   LONDON   PARIS

ART DIRECTION **ANDREAS PORSCH**

FOR THE ENGLISH EDITION
EDITOR **MEREDITH WOLF SCHIZER**
DESIGNER **MOLLY SHIELDS**
TYPESETTER **KEVIN CALLAHAN**
PRODUCTION MANAGER **LOU BILKA**

First edition
10 9 8 7 6 5 4 3 2 1

Library of Congress Cataloging-in-Publication Data
Rum drinks and havanas : Cuba classics / concept and recipes by
  Ernst Lechthaler ; photography by Amiel Pretsch ; text by August F.
  Winkler. — 1st ed.
        p.   cm.
    Includes index.
    ISBN 0-7892-0527-0
    1. Cocktails.   2. Rum—Cuba.   I. Lechthaler, Ernst.   II. Pretsch,
  Amiel.   III. Winkler, August F.
  TX951.R86   1999
  641.2'59'097291—dc21   98-40452

Contents

Foreword

MY FRIENDS ASK ME SO WHAT'S SO SPECIAL ABOUT CUBA. I CLOSE MY EYES, LISTEN TO MY HEART, AND REPLY THAT IT'S SOMETHING YOU CAN'T EXPLAIN BY SIMPLY RANKING ITS CHARMS; YOU CAN ONLY SENSE IT, LIKE AN ENCHANTING FAIRY TALE.

TO ME, CUBA IS . . .

- LYING ON THE BEACH AND DAYDREAMING

- SIPPING A DAIQUIRI IN THE FLORIDITA, FAR FROM THE CARES OF THE WORLD

- WATCHING ATTRACTIVE WOMEN AS THEY REGISTER YOUR GAZE WITH A BRIEF LIFT OF THEIR EYES, THEN SWIVEL THEIR HIPS ALL THE MORE COQUETTISHLY

- INHALING THE RICH BOUQUET OF SPICES, HONEY, RARE WOODS, LEATHER, HERBS, NUTS, SMOKE, CHOCOLATE, AND FADED ROSES IN A CIGAR FACTORY

- SMOKING A COHIBA ESPLENDIDOS, A SANCHO FROM SANCHO PANZA, OR A MONTECRISTO NO. 2—THE SO-CALLED TORPEDO—AND BEING GRATEFUL TO THE WOMEN WHO ROLL THOSE MIRACLES WITH SUCH ARTISTRY

- STROLLING THROUGH THE OLD CITY OF HAVANA AND APPRECIATING ITS AMAZING HISTORY AND ITS SENSE OF PRIDE

- EXPERIENCING HEART-WRENCHING SOCIAL CHAOS AND YET FINDING EXHILARATION IN IT

- SENSING THE UNQUENCHABLE HOPE FOR BETTER TIMES

MY FRIENDS OBJECT THAT I AM OVERDOING IT A LITTLE. PERHAPS, I ADMIT. BUT THIS MUCH IS CERTAIN: HAVANA IS THE MOST JOYFUL CITY IN THE WORLD. THERE PEOPLE RECOGNIZE THAT A FOOL'S STONE IS NOT SO VERY DIFFERENT FROM THE PHILOSOPHER'S STONE.

Balm
of the
Spirit

THE IMMORTAL HEMINGWAY ON RUM:

"HE DRANK IT AGAINST THE POVERTY, AGAINST
THE FILTH, AGAINST THE DUST OF 400 YEARS
AND THE RUNNY NOSES OF THE CHILDREN,
AGAINST THE BROKEN PALMS ALONG THE
STREET AND THE ROOFS NAILED TOGETHER
FROM TIN CANS."

What Is Cuban Rum?

A London wine merchant had invited some friends, all of them connoisseurs, to what he told them was a blind tasting of noble brandies, but he had smuggled Havana Club's Gran Reserva, a fifteen-year-old rum, in among the vintage Cognacs and malt whiskys. Only two of the twelve participants correctly identified the pirate as rum; the others ranked it with the best Cognacs and malts. And these were experts, not ordinary, casual drinkers.

It is true that rum is generally misunderstood outside the Caribbean. People have a vague idea that it is required for a number of mixed drinks, they like using it in grog or adding it to their tea, and they use it as a marinade for fruit and as a flavoring for baked goods; but scarcely anyone knows how wonderful a rum that has been aged in the barrel can taste if you drink it neat. To be sure, rum's aftertaste is not particularly impressive. On the other hand, a first-class rum presents the nose and the palate with a greater range of nuanced aromas than almost any other spirit. Traditional seamen's songs—rum was long considered the typical sailor's drink—as well as cheap dilutions and a general absence of enlightenment are responsible for rum's poor reputation.

Rums are not all alike. Their taste varies widely depending on where and how they were distilled. The microclimate and soil in which sugarcane is grown in Cuba are not the same as those of Jamaica or Haiti. It makes a difference whether rum is distilled from pure sugarcane sap or from molasses, the syrup that is left after the sugar is filtered out. The length of the fermentation process, the choice of additives, the quality of the yeast, the distilling technique, and the manner and duration of the distillate's aging all greatly influence a rum's character and aroma.

More often than not, the "gold of the Caribbean" is derived from molasses, a thick, dark syrup that is a byproduct of the refinery. This extremely sweet "honey" is thinned with water—otherwise it could not be fermented, due to its high sugar content—then fermented with a special yeast. To give the result aroma, it is common to add spices (vanilla beans, cinnamon, cloves), dried fruits (raisins, pineapple), or other substances (peach leaves, acacia bark, plum extract). Every distillery has its own secret flavorings.

When first distilled, rum is colorless and raw tasting. At this stage it is necessary to decide whether it will remain clear or be given a golden-brown color, which comes either from aging in wooden barrels or the addition of caramel or sugar color.

Rum is essentially divided into three basic groups:

1. **White, or light.** After distilling, aged in stainless steel tanks, which add no color. Light with a dry aroma. Used as a base for mixed drinks.

2. **Medium.** Golden or light brown in color. The darker color results from aging in oak barrels—preferably barrels previously used in the aging of bourbon. The wood gives off coloring agents as well as sweetish, spicy aromas. Ideal for use in cocktails, fruit marinades, and baking.

3. **Dark brown and heavy.** Deep gold or dark brown in color. A full-bodied type with somewhat sweet and spicy aromas. Aged

RUM, THE BLESSED OFFSPRING OF SUGARCANE, IS COM-
MONLY KNOWN TO BE EFFECTIVE IN CASES OF FLU, LOVE,
HOMESICKNESS, AND CHILLS, AND IT PROVIDES RELIEF
FROM THE INSIPID COCKTAIL. BUT ONLY A FEW KNOW THAT
IT WAS COLUMBUS, WITH HIS INTRODUCTION OF SUGAR-
CANE TO CUBA ON HIS SECOND VOYAGE, WHO SET THE
STAGE FOR THE PRODUCTION OF CARIBBEAN RUM.

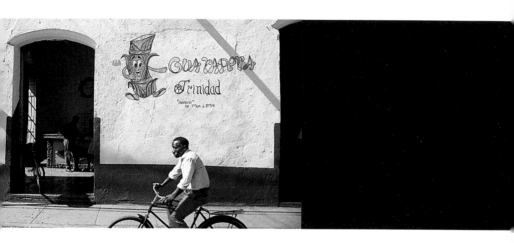

for a long time in oak barrels. Richly nuanced flavor even when
drunk straight. The perfect accompaniment to a great Havana
cigar. First-class rum with a complex aroma. Depending on where
it was produced, you may associate its smell and taste with honey,
caramel, vanilla, raisins, tropical fruits, spices, leather, tobacco,
dried plums, oranges, or chocolate.

THE CRADLE

THERE'S NAUGHT, NO DOUBT, SO MUCH THE SPIRIT CALMS
AS RUM AND TRUE RELIGION. **LORD BYRON,** *DON JUAN*

Rum must have been produced in
Cuba if it is to be called Cuban rum.
Havana Club, the national brand
established in 1878, is Cuba's only
international rum and is one of the
best in the world. This "Cuban single
cane" is distilled in Santa Cruz del
Norte, a coastal village east of
Havana. It comes in various grades
and ages:

Havana Club "Silver Dry": White,
aged roughly 2 years in oak barrels.
75 proof. Ideal basis for tall drinks
and cocktails. Full, with delicate
floral and fruity notes.

Havana Club "Añejo 3 Años": Gold,
aged 3 years in oak barrels. 80 proof.
Excellently suited for rum cocktails.
Mild, mature, and slightly sweet.

Havana Club "Añejo 5 Años": Dark
gold, aged 5 years in oak barrels.
80 proof. Balanced, fruity, spicy,
and delicately sweet, with a touch
of citrus, caramel, and vanilla. Mild
and refined. A true delight taken
neat with a cigar.

Havana Club "Añejo 7 Años": Dark
brown, aged 7 years in oak barrels.
80 proof. A mature, rounded rum with
a rich aroma of spices, dried fruits,
vanilla, and honey. Elegant, with a
sweet piquancy. Delicious when drunk
neat from a brandy snifter. Perfect
with Havana cigars.

[THE] DAIQUIRIS HAD NO TASTE OF ALCOHOL AND FELT, AS YOU DRANK THEM, THE WAY DOWNHILL GLACIER SKIING FEELS RUNNING THROUGH POWDER SNOW AND, AFTER THE SIXTH AND EIGHTH, FELT LIKE DOWNHILL GLACIER SKIING FEELS WHEN YOU ARE RUNNING UNROPED.

ERNEST HEMINGWAY, *ISLANDS IN THE STREAM*, 1970

RIGHT: HEMINGWAY'S WORKROOM IN HIS HOUSE IN THE SOUTHEAST OF HAVANA (FINCA VIGIA, SAN FRANCESCO DE PAULA).

BELOW: ONE OF THE THREE BARS IN THE RESTAURANT 1830 (AT THE INTERSECTION OF ALMENDORE).

MOJITO

1 oz. (30 ml) freshly squeezed lime juice
6–8 fresh leaves of *erba buena* or other mint
⅔ oz. (15 ml) cane syrup or 2 barspoons white cane sugar
2 oz. (60 ml) Havana Club white rum
1 dash mineral water

Combine the lime juice, mint leaves, and sugar in a glass.
Crush the mint leaves with a pestle. Add rum. Fill the
glass with ice cubes. Top with mineral water and stir
briefly. Garnish with a sprig of mint and serve with a straw.

LEFT: IN THE BODEGUITA DEL MEDIO, HOME OF THE MOJITO.

CUBA LIBRE

2 oz. (60 ml) white rum

¼ lime

cola

Place ice cubes in a glass and add rum. Squeeze lime over it (roughly ½ oz. [10 ml] juice) and drop the lime into the glass. Fill with cola. Stir.

FROZEN DAIQUIRI

THIS DRINK IS ALSO CALLED A DAIQUIRI FRAPPÉ OR—SINCE IT WAS CREATED IN HAVANA'S FLORIDITA, ONE OF HEMINGWAY'S FAVORITE BARS—A FLORIDITA DAIQUIRI.

¾ oz. (20 ml) freshly squeezed
lime juice

½ oz. (10 ml) sugarcane syrup or
1 barspoon white cane sugar

2 oz. (60 ml) Havana Club
white rum

dash maraschino liqueur

Blend all ingredients with a
glassful of crushed ice in a
mixer on high speed. Pour
into a chilled glass. Serve
with a short, thick straw.

FRUIT DAIQUIRIS

Preparation as for the Frozen Daiquiri, p. 23.

PEACH DAIQUIRI

¾ oz. (20 ml) freshly squeezed lime juice
1 barspoon white cane sugar or ½ oz. (10 ml) sugarcane syrup
1¾ oz. (50 ml) Havana Club white rum
½ oz. (10 ml) peach brandy
¼ ripe peach

STRAWBERRY DAIQUIRI

¾ oz. (20 ml) freshly squeezed lime juice
⅔ oz. (15 ml) strawberry syrup
2 oz. (60 ml) Havana Club white rum
5 barspoons crushed strawberries (roughly three
medium-sized berries)

STRAWBERRY DAIQUIRI

BANANA DAIQUIRI

¾ oz. (20 ml) freshly squeezed lime juice
⅔ oz. (15 ml) banana syrup
2 oz. (60 ml) white rum
¼ ripe banana

LECHTHALER'S BANANA DAIQUIRI

¾ oz. (20 ml) freshly squeezed lime juice
⅔ oz. (15 ml) banana syrup
1 oz. (30 ml) white rum
1 oz. (30 ml) Havana Club brown rum (7-year-old)
¼ ripe banana

DAIQUIRI CHICLET

5 dashes (2 barspoons) freshly squeezed lime juice
1 barspoon white cane sugar or ½ oz. (10 ml) sugarcane syrup
¾ oz. (20 ml) peppermint liqueur
¾ oz. (20 ml) banana liqueur
1½ oz. (40 ml) white rum

DAIQUIRI REBELDE

¾ oz. (20 ml) freshly squeezed lime juice
½ oz. (10 ml) sugarcane syrup or 1 barspoon white cane sugar
¾ oz. (20 ml) peppermint liqueur
2 oz. (60 ml) white rum

DAIQUIRI REBELDE

DAIQUIRI DON ROLANDO (named for the bartender at the Floridita)

¾ oz. (20 ml) freshly squeezed lime juice
2 barspoons white cane sugar
2 fresh mint leaves
5 dashes green crème de menthe
2 oz. (60 ml) white rum

DAIQUIRI DE PINA

1 slice ripe pineapple (roughly ½ in. [1 cm] thick, without rind and core)
¾ oz. (20 ml) freshly squeezed lime juice
2 barspoons white cane sugar or ⅔ oz. (15 ml) sugarcane syrup
2 oz. (60 ml) white rum

DAIQUIRI

1 oz. (30 ml) freshly squeezed lime juice

⅔ oz. (15 ml) sugarcane syrup or 2 barspoons
white cane sugar

1¾ oz. (50 ml) Havana Club white rum

    Shake with ice cubes and strain into a chilled glass.

VARIANT

LECHTHALER'S DAIQUIRI

1 oz. (30 ml) freshly squeezed lemon juice

⅔ oz. (15 ml) sugarcane syrup or 2 barspoons
white cane sugar

1 oz. (30 ml) white rum

1 oz. (30 ml) brown rum (7-year-old)

    Shake with ice cubes and strain into a chilled glass.

DAIQUIRI MULATA

¾ oz. (20 ml) freshly squeezed lime juice
½ oz. (10 ml) sugarcane syrup or 1 barspoon white cane sugar
¾ oz. (20 ml) brown crème de cacao
2 oz. (60 ml) Havana Club brown rum (7-year-old)
5 dashes maraschino liqueur

Mix thoroughly on high in a blender with almost a glassful of crushed ice. Pour into a chilled glass. Serve with a straw.

DAIQUIRI PAPA HEMINGWAY

THIS DRINK IS ALSO CALLED AN ERNEST HEMINGWAY SPECIAL, ONE OF HIS FAVORITE DRINKS. HE PREFERRED IT WITHOUT SUGAR AND WITH A BIT MORE RUM.

¾ oz. (20 ml) freshly
squeezed lime juice

1½ oz. (40 ml) fresh
grapefruit juice

½ oz. (10 ml) maraschino
liqueur

3 oz. (80 ml) (at least)
white Cuban rum

Mix thoroughly on high in a
blender with a glassful of crushed
ice. Pour into the chilled glass.
Serve with a straw.

PRESIDENTE
(PICTURED AT RIGHT)

1½ oz. (40 ml) Havana Club white rum
½ oz. (10 ml) extra-dry vermouth
½ oz. (10 ml) vermouth rosso
¼ oz. (5 ml) triple sec

> Stir in a mixer with ice cubes, then strain into a chilled
> glass. Garnish with a maraschino cherry (without stem).
> Squeeze the zest of an orange and drop it into the glass.

VARIANT

EL PRESIDENTE

add
1 dash freshly squeezed lemon juice
1 dash Grenadine syrup

> Ingredients and preparation like the Presidente.
> Do not garnish.

RIGHT: HEMINGWAY'S REGULAR STOOL IN THE FLORIDITA,
RESERVED PERMANENTLY.

CANCHANCHARA

1 oz. (30 ml) freshly squeezed lime juice
¾ oz. (20 ml) liquid honey
2 oz. (60 ml) white rum
a shot of uncarbonated water (if desired)

Pour ingredients into a glass. Stir well until the honey is
completely dissolved. Add ice cubes. Stir again. Garnish
with a slice of lime.

GUARAPO CON RON

(PICTURED AT LEFT)

4 oz. (120 ml) sugarcane sap, freshly squeezed
2 oz. (60 ml) white Cuban rum
¼ lime

Pour the sugarcane sap and rum into the glass. Add ice
cubes. Squeeze the lime over the drink (approximately
½ oz. [10 ml] juice) and drop in the lime. Stir briefly.

SAOCO

2¾ oz. (100 ml) coconut milk
1¾ oz. (50 ml) white rum

Stir ingredients into a glass with ice cubes.

THE DAIQUIRI (LEFT) AND THE MOJITO (RIGHT) ARE CUBA'S NATIONAL DRINKS. THE MOJITO CALLS FOR *ERBA BUENA*, A TYPE OF MINT.

Homage to the Bar

On your left as you enter the Floridita, also known as the birth-place of the daiquiri, you'll notice that the last barstool against the wall is chained off like the Mona Lisa in the Louvre. The corner is consecrated, like a temple, to Ernest "Papa" Hemingway, a regular from the old days who continues to be the bar's great draw. Crowds of tourists come in every day to see where the quintessential macho drank his daiquiri. They then perch like chickens on the stools, order 7-Up, take photos, and fill the space with their chatter. But still it's worth a visit, for you can have a great conversation about Hemingway, times past, and cocktails with the red-coated head bartender, Rolando Quinones.

He'll mix you a daiquiri the way Hemingway drank them, with no sugar and a double dose of rum. Quinones has also created a daiquiri of his own using crème de menthe and with two mint leaves as a garnish. Here we call it the Don Rolando. Fried manioc slices taste especially good with it. And try a Robusto from Cohiba along with a rum aged in wooden barrels—a harmony of pleasures.

Anyone who wants to really experience Cuba, to get a true sense of the land and its people instead of simply lying on the beach or collecting a bunch of dry statistics, has to visit its bars. The bar is to Cuba what the coffeehouse is to Vienna: it's a place where you feel at home, even though you're not. Cuban bars are theaters; people talking, listening, meditating, and sometimes drinking their way past a reality that doesn't always have a silver lining.

A bar, like no other place on earth, lets you do just that. You want solitude without being alone? You want company but nobody special? You want to drink something, but not just anything? The answer is always a bar. And Havana is the capital of bars.

The most famous bar is the one in the movies: Rick's Café Americaine in Casablanca. But in the Floridita, where the best daiquiris are made, you can also see the best real-life film scripts being written—or even learn that Hemingway never said, "Mi daiquiri en el Floridita y mi mojito en la Bodeguita del Medio." This much-publicized quote at the Bodeguita del Medio comes from Fernando B. Campoamor, a journalist and friend of Papa's who still lives in Havana at eighty-two. Thirty-six years ago, he suggested to the Bodeguita's owner by way of a joke that if he wanted to become famous he needed a quote from Hemingway.

In the Bodeguita del Medio you have to signal to the man behind the bar that he can let the rum flow a bit longer into your mojito. That's the curse of tourism. In less famous Cuban bars you can be relatively certain of getting what you pay for. The best bars tend to be fairly conservative in their offerings.

Although modern recipes can be altogether delightful, and any enlightened soul is bound to welcome certain reforms, arcane contemporary mixtures have their place in the scene bar but never in the classic bar, the holy grail of high-alcohol-content drinking culture.

THE BAR IS TO CUBA WHAT THE COFFEE HOUSE IS TO VIENNA: IT'S A PLACE WHERE YOU FEEL AT HOME, EVEN THOUGH YOU'RE NOT.

BARTENDERS ARE BORN, NOT MADE. THEY ARE ENTERTAINERS,
FATHER CONFESSORS, AND PHILOSOPHERS ALL IN ONE.
YOU CAN TALK WITH THEM ABOUT GOD AND WORLD EVENTS
AND DEBATE WHETHER ANGOSTURA REALLY BELONGS IN
A COLLINS OR WHETHER THE BROTH FOR A BULL SHOT
SHOULD BE DEFATTED.

The true barfly acknowledges only a few real drinks. At the top of the hierarchy are classic cocktails, rum, malt, Cognac, and champagne. Everything else is tipple. Anyone who says to a bartender, "Make me something pretty, something colorful, you know what I mean," might as well visit a juice bar. No bartender worthy of the title is likely to think of himself as a health jerk. Those who do confuse Angostura with Maggi, garnish everything with the unholy cherry, turn every drink into a production, and mix a Quarter Deck with vermouth, even though every connoisseur knows that it's supposed to be made with a teaspoon lime juice, one-third sherry, and two-thirds rum.

CUBA COLADA

4 oz. (120 ml) pineapple juice

1 oz. (30 ml) coconut cream

2 oz. (60 ml) white rum

Mix all ingredients in a shaker with ice cubes. Strain into a glass one-third full of crushed ice. Garnish with a quarter slice of fresh pineapple and a maraschino cherry with stem, if desired. Serve with a straw.

Colada variation: **4 oz. (120 ml) pineapple juice, 1 oz. (30 ml) coconut cream, ¾ oz. (20 ml) cream, 1 oz. (30 ml) white rum, 1 oz. (30 ml) brown rum.** Prepare as above.

CUBAN SIDE CAR

1 oz. (30 ml) freshly squeezed lime juice
1 oz. (30 ml) triple sec
1 oz. (30 ml) Havana Club white rum

Mix in a shaker with ice cubes. Strain into a
chilled glass.

CUBAN RUM PUNCH

¾ oz. (20 ml) lime juice
½ oz. (10 ml) grenadine syrup
3 oz. (80 ml) orange juice
1¾ oz. (50 ml) Havana Club brown rum

Mix in a shaker with ice cubes. Strain into a glass one-third full of crushed ice. Add a pinch of nutmeg. Garnish with an orange slice and a maraschino cherry. Serve with a straw.

Rum Punch variation: ½ oz. (10 ml) freshly squeezed lime juice, 1½ oz. (40 ml) orange juice, 3 oz. (80 ml) pineapple juice, ¼ oz. (5 ml) grenadine syrup, 1 oz. (30 ml) white rum, 1 oz. (30 ml) brown rum (7-year-old). Prepare as above.

LONG & SHORT OF RUM

RON COLLINS

1 oz. (30 ml) freshly squeezed lime juice
3 barspoons white cane sugar
1¾ oz. (50 ml) white rum
seltzer

Pour the lime juice, sugar, and rum (in this order) into a collins glass filled with ice cubes. Top with seltzer. Stir briefly. Garnish with a slice of lime and two maraschino cherries. Serve with a straw.

ISLA DE PINOS

1½ oz. (40 ml) grapefruit juice
1 barspoon cane sugar
5 dashes grenadine syrup
2 oz. (60 ml) white rum

Mix in a blender with crushed ice. Pour into a chilled glass. Garnish with a half slice of grapefruit on the edge of the glass. Serve with a straw.

NACIONAL

¾ oz. (20 ml) pineapple juice
¾ oz. (20 ml) apricot brandy
1½ oz. (40 ml) Havana Club Old Gold
1–2 dashes freshly squeezed lime juice

Mix with ice in a shaker. Strain into a chilled glass.

HAVANA SPECIAL

1¾ oz. (50 ml) pineapple juice
5 dashes (1 barspoon) sugarcane syrup
5 dashes (1 barspoon) maraschino liqueur
1¾ oz. (50 ml) white rum

Mix with ice in a shaker. Strain into a chilled glass. Garnish with a maraschino cherry on a stick laid across the glass.

RON COLLINS   MARY PICKFORD

MARY PICKFORD

Ingredients and preparation as for a Havana Special, using grenadine syrup instead of sugarcane syrup.

No garnish.

CHAPARRA

2 oz. (60 ml) white rum
¾ oz. (20 ml) vermouth rosso

Stir with ice in a mixing glass. Strain into a chilled glass. Add a squeeze of lemon zest and drop it into the glass.

CUBAN SPECIAL

½ oz. (10 ml) freshly squeezed lime juice
¾ oz. (20 ml) pineapple juice
½ oz. (10 ml) triple sec
1¾ oz. (50 ml) white rum

Mix in a shaker. Strain into a chilled glass.

PERIODISTA

½ oz. (10 ml) freshly squeezed lime juice
1 barspoon powdered sugar
½ oz. (10 ml) apricot brandy
½ oz. (10 ml) triple sec
1½ oz. (40 ml) white rum

Mix in a shaker. Strain into a chilled glass. Squeeze in lime zest and drop it into the glass.

SMOKE MARTINI

DRINKS TO ENJOY WITH A CIGAR, CREATED BY ERNST LECHTHALER

HABANOS HAVANA

1½ oz. (40 ml) gin
¾ oz. (20 ml) Havana Club
brown rum (7-year-old)

Stir with ice in a mixing glass.
Strain into a chilled glass.
Garnish with a maraschino
cherry and zest of lime.

1 oz. (30 ml) lime juice
1¾ oz. (50 ml) Havana Club
brown rum
½ oz. (10 ml) sugarcane syrup
¾ oz. (20 ml) triple sec

Mix with ice in a shaker. Strain
into a chilled glass. Garnish with
a maraschino cherry.

The
Drapery
of the
Soul

What Makes the Havana Unique?

It was a picture of sublime, even erotic grace. The woman lit her cigar with such surrender, such practiced assurance, slowly rotating the tip above the flame. That's the way to do it; you don't want to overheat a cigar, especially a Havana. If you do, you do violence to the aroma—it's like rubbing sandpaper over silk. Only after the tip was glowing all the way around did the woman place the Cohiba Lanceros in her mouth. The Lanceros, a Gran Panetela, seven-and-a-half inches (19.2 cm) long and five-eighths of an inch (1.5 cm) in diameter, is also known as the Chanel No. 5 of Havanas. The men watched respectfully, for even the strong have been known to be broken by a cudgel like this. As chance would have it, there had been an article in the previous day's paper saying that more and more women and young men are taking up cigars. That's an encouraging trend, for the cigar reflects a peaceful, contented approach to life. The cigarette is all about haste, but the cigar stands for calm and meditation. Bismarck got it right in his response to a French counterpart who expressed surprise at his lighting up a cigar during the peace negotiations in 1871. "You see," the Iron Chancellor explained, "a cigar gently calms the spirit without impairing your ability to think. It's a distraction. You can't help but watch the curling blue smoke, and there's something fascinating about it that makes everything seem reconciled. You feel wonderful, your eyes have something to look at and your sense of smell is rewarded."

Just as with wine, the type of cigar you choose, whether long or short, thick or slender, heavy or light, depends on your mood, on the amount of time you have, and on your finances. In its aromatic richness a Havana is comparable to the fruity fullness and refinement of a superb red burgundy. Of all the cigars in the world, it has the richest, most complex aroma. No other cigar, no matter how beautifully wrapped, has the deep, elegant flavor of a pure Cuban cigar.

The secret lies in the warm soil of Pinar del Rio, Cuba's major tobacco province, where the incomparable leaf for the best cigars is grown

in reddish clay in the region known as Vuelta Abajo. Even the special microclimate plays a role. Heinrich Villiger, a Swiss importer of Cuban cigars who supplies Germany with Havanas, points to another factor: "In Cuba they have the most experience." He agrees that climate and soil composition are the main things that make Cuban tobacco world-class, pointing to tests in which Cuban tobacco seeds were planted in the Dominican Republic, in Nicaragua, and in Mexico. The result was astonishing: the tobaccos harvested were completely different. For Villiger, the special quality of Cuban tobacco is also the result of centuries-old tradition: "Nobody understands growing, fermentation, and preparation of cigar tobacco as well as [Cubans] do."

Even in Cuba, of course, there are cigars, and then there are *cigars*. There is a world of difference between a Montecristo A and a Robusto from Cohiba. The former, over nine inches (23.5 cm) long and a hefty three-quarters of an inch (1.9 cm) in diameter, provides roughly two hours of smoking pleasure. The Robusto, nearly five inches (12.4 cm) long and

three-quarters of an inch (2 cm) in diameter, is also a delight to smoke but doesn't last as long. Among Cuban cigars there are queens and—to put it charitably—housemaids: cigars that glow nicely but that just aren't first-class, either because the harvest was less than ideal or short cuts were taken in production.

You need to be discriminating in your buying and pay close attention until you find the right cigar for you. Be especially wary of rip-offs, cheaply produced forgeries. A perfectly aged cigar should have a soft sheen, and it should be pliant and surrender to gentle pressure without crackling. When you open the wooden box, the aroma should be intoxicating and the outer leaf a delight to the eye, neither strongly ribbed nor too pale, spotty, lacquered looking, or irregular.

IF THEY DON'T ALLOW CIGAR SMOKING IN HEAVEN, I DON'T WANT TO GO THERE. **MARK TWAIN**

Dry cigars develop a sharp, biting taste, which is why it is advisable to buy cigars only in specialty shops that have humidor cabinets. If you watch out, you won't be fooled. And when the cigar goes up in smoke, as it is meant to do, it will immediately transport you into a state of deep relaxation. Armchair psychologists see the cigar as a kind of pacifier for grown-ups, a lolly for the needy soul and a security prop for appearances in public. Perhaps, but on the other hand they may be simply envious of those blessed with a greater talent for enjoying themselves. It was Sigmund Freud, after all, who impishly responded to a woman who wanted to see something sinister in his fondness for big Coronas: "Sometimes a cigar is just a cigar."

A CIGAR POPULATES THE SOLITUDE WITH
A THOUSAND PLEASANT IMAGES.
GEORGE SAND

The Cohiba

The Cohiba, Cuba's number-one cigar, is already a legend, though it is only thirty years old. The name simply means "tobacco"; it was the word used by the original inhabitants of the island for the rolled leaves smoked in special ceremonies by chieftains and priests. Originally the Cohiba was reserved for government officials, diplomats, and important guests. It was only in 1982 that the brand was released for worldwide sale. At that time it came in only three formats: Lanceros, Coronas Especiales, and Panetelas. Three additional formats were introduced in 1989: Espléndidos, Robustos, and Exquisitos. Finally in 1992, within what was called the Cohiba Collection, five additional formats were created under the name Linea 1492, commemorating Christopher Columbus's discovery of America and with it, tobacco. They were named after each of the intervening centuries, from Siglo I through Siglo V.

What makes the Cohiba a cult cigar? For one thing, it is the first cigar to have been developed entirely by Cubans since the revolution. Skillful marketing, emphasizing its transformation from an exclusive product to one shared with the people of the world, portrays it as something very special. Finally, the Cohiba is considered to be the result of Cuba's most lavish production. According to Emilia Tamayo, the demanding director of the Cohiba manufacturing plant El Laguito in Havana, "Cohibas are the best of the best." Only superior tobaccos are used— that is, leaves graded select. Moreover, the tobacco is subjected to three fermentations, instead of the two that are standard for other brands. The Cohiba producers feel that the third fermentation reduces the amount of tar and nicotine without sacrificing aroma, resulting in a gentler cigar that is ready to smoke the minute it is placed on the market.

HOW TO TREAT CIGARS

Storage: Only perfectly stored cigars are good cigars. They should have a soft sheen (not as though powdered), and you ought to be able to squeeze them without any crackling sounds. The ideal storage place for them is a humidor set at a humidity of 70 to 75 percent. A wine cellar is fine as long as it is well

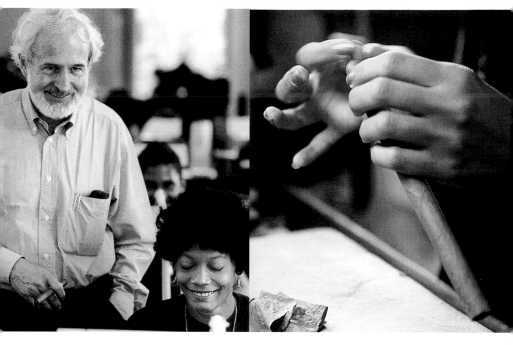

ABOVE: HEINRICH VILLIGER TESTS THE QUALITY OF HIS CIGARS.

ventilated, dark, and sufficiently damp. Havanas that have become dry will recover in a humidor.

Lighting: Use a flame with no odor only. No benzene lighters, no candles, and matches only after the smell of sulfur has dissipated. Cedar wood looks great, but the flame is too restless. A gas lighter is best. First carefully light the tip, then draw gently, taking care to achieve an even glow. The cigar should not be overheated. The hotter it becomes, the more biting the taste—one reason for not rushing things.

Band: Remove it or not? A question of no importance. Some take it off because they want their cigar naked, or because they don't want to smoke an advertisement. Others leave it on, fearing that they could damage the outer leaf when sliding it off.

Ash: How long do you leave it on? Don't overdo, but the ash has an important function: it protects the fire and encourages even burning. A cigar with ash on it smokes cooler. Don't just knock it off, but stroke it off gently.

Relighting: No problem with cigars that have been smoked only halfway down. Beyond the second third, forget it. When lighting, do not draw, but rather slowly rotate the tip above the flame (not in the flame) and light. Then carefully take a first draw.

Extinguishing: Don't stub out the glowing cigar but simply leave it in the ashtray. It will go out by itself.

COHIBA PROFILES

Panetelas: 4½ in. (11.5 cm) long; ⅜ in. (1 cm) in diameter. Gentle aroma, becoming somewhat sharper at the end—typical of small cigars. Slender format, ideal for theater intermissions or for a morning smoke.

Exquisitos: 4⅞ in. (12.5 cm) long; ½ in. (1.4 cm) in diameter. Gently spicy, aromatic, velvety, light, and delicate. A cigar for every time of day.

Coronas Especiales: 5⅞ in. (15.2 cm) long; ⅝ in. (1.5 cm) in diameter. The little sister of the Lanceros. Floral spiciness, fruity, rather light structure, occasionally somewhat bitter at the end. A cigar for in-between.

Lanceros: 7½ in. (19.2 cm) long; ⅜ in. (1.5 cm) in diameter. Gran Panetela format—for many, the top cigar of the entire collection. Delicately spicy aroma, dense but refined. Elegant cigar, ideal after a fine meal and for relaxing over tea or port.

Robustos: 4⅞ in. (12.4 cm) long; ¾ in. (2 cm) in diameter. Short, thick, and with a grandiose aroma. A high-quality cigar with a strong, full bouquet. Spicy, velvety, fiery. The ideal cigar after a heavy lunch or at teatime, when there isn't time for a larger format.

Espléndidos: 7 in. (17.8 cm) long; ¾ in. (1.9 cm) in diameter. Gran Corona format. Strong flavor, concentrated, spicy aroma. Thick and complex, yet delicate to the end. A large cigar that com-

pletes an elegant dinner or provides, along with a glass of port or aged rum, relaxation in front of the fire.

Siglo I: 4 in. (10.2 cm) long; ⅝ in. (1.6 cm) in diameter. The shortest Cohiba with a diameter like a large-format cigar. Pleasantly light and spicy, delicate aroma, a sort of appetizer among the Cohibas, attractive for a short break from work.

Siglo II: 5 in. (12.9 cm) long; ⅝ in. (1.7 cm) in diameter. Unspectacular but popular Petit Corona format. Gently spicy aroma with a light coffee note. Mild character. Always suitable, ideal for first-time smokers.

Siglo III: 6 in. (15.5 cm) long; ⅝ in. (1.7 cm) in diameter. Somewhat longer than a Corona. Velvety spice, delicate smoke. Elegant cigar. Suitable for after meals and as a digestive.

Siglo IV: 5⅝ in. (14.3 cm) long; ¾ in. (1.8 cm) in diameter. The Cohiba with the greatest diameter. Spicy aroma of cinnamon and sandalwood. Opulent but smooth. A richly nuanced cigar for after a large meal. Requires a long time.

Siglo V: 6⅝ in. (17 cm) long; ⅝ in. (1.7 cm) in diameter. Strong, full aroma with spicy undertones; richly nuanced, dense structure. Ideal as the conclusion to a great culinary experience or at the fireplace with port, rum, whisky, or a fine Cognac. Not for Sunday smokers.

A GOOD HAVANA IS ONE OF THE BEST THINGS I KNOW.
WHEN I WAS YOUNG AND VERY POOR, I ONLY SMOKED
CIGARS WHEN SOMEBODY OFFERED ME ONE, AND I
DETERMINED THAT IF I EVER HAD MONEY I WOULD ENJOY
ONE EVERY DAY AFTER LUNCH AND AFTER DINNER. THAT
IS THE ONLY INTENTION FROM MY YOUTH THAT I HAVE
CARRIED OUT, THE ONLY PIPE-DREAM THAT WAS FULFILLED
WITHOUT BEING A DISAPPOINTMENT.
SOMERSET MAUGHAM

A

Caribbean

Carnival

Cuban Sidelights

IT BEGINS WITH A SUDDEN STIRRING IN YOUR BODY, LIKE
A NEED FOR LOVE. IT'S SIMPLE: YOU NEED TO GET AWAY,
IMMEDIATELY. PERHAPS TO CUBA.

High time to stroll through Havana again, to drink a genuine
daiquiri in one of its bars, the salons of Cuba, to let yourself be swept
along by the salsa, and to be infected by the joy of the people. Havana is
the metropolis of survival, a myth from a lost time. Back then, in the belle
époque and the decades that followed, people used to call Havana the Paris
of the Caribbean. Wealthy idlers, American gangsters, European dandies,
writers, artists—all converged on Havana. Who now remembers that the
Met used to make regular appearances in Havana, or that Erich Kleiber
conducted the local symphony orchestra?

All of that is past. Aside from a few yellowed photographs, all that
remains of those luxurious, corrupt, and glittering times are the memories.
Today the plaster is crumbling off the art deco, and behind the barricaded
facades families are living without running water or electricity. The poverty
is obvious; those who don't have dollars go without. There are plenty of
doctors, but little aspirin. Children beg, women offer themselves, and men
try to sell you a whole range of black-market goods, from imitation cigars to
homemade rum. The ideal has become grotesque: *morbidezza* in Caribbean.

Yet today Havana is bustling once again. Traffic pulses in a collective frenzy. At intersections stand lines of people. The streets are filled with automobile fossils—Chevys, Fords, Buicks, and Cadillacs from the 1950s that rattle and squeak, some held together with rope. The sidewalks overflow with white people, black people, brown people. The women are as beautiful as goddesses, but often more approachable.

One wonders where the people get their strength, their incredible, laudable energy. In their misery, they can still laugh about it. The men carry themselves with dignity, the women with graceful self-assurance. Their talent for improvising a festival out of seeming nothingness at the drop of a hat is unparalleled.

BACK IN THE BELLE ÉPOQUE AND THE DECADES THAT
FOLLOWED, PEOPLE USED TO CALL HAVANA THE PARIS
OF THE CARIBBEAN.

THE SIDEWALKS ARE FULL OF WHITE PEOPLE,
BLACK PEOPLE, BROWN PEOPLE. THE WOMEN ARE
AS BEAUTIFUL AS GODDESSES. . . .

No city map in the world, with the possible exception of that of Port of France in Trinidad, makes such melodic reading as Havana's. Palacio de Aldemar, Paseo de Marti, Esperanza, Muralia, Malecón—these are swinging, especially along the shore promenade where lovers meet. Naturally, exploring Havana takes time. You cannot expect the country to simply introduce itself, you have to make the approach yourself.

Life begins every day at sunrise. The city sparkles most colorfully on the edge between daylight and darkness. The best way to deal with time in Havana—in fact everywhere in Cuba—is to forget it. Then you're free. Don't set any goals that have to be accomplished by a certain time. Just walk, not necessarily to get anywhere but just to be where you are. Watch, listen, and feel—that's the best way to experience the island, and Havana, as it lives and breathes.

THE CITY SPARKLES MOST COLORFULLY ON THE EDGE BETWEEN DAYLIGHT AND DARKNESS.

Cuba's Carnival

The drums beat, the pipes trill, the trumpets blare like the ones outside Jericho. It is Carnival. The miles-long parade winds through the broad boulevards. The dancers outdo themselves in trancelike rhythms.

Salsa, rumba, masks. The whole city dances. On these days a love of life is expressed ecstatically. Dance, sing, and forget. The music is loud, the rhythm infectious. It is neither a coda to the old life nor a switch to the future, just the unthinking celebration of the moment.

Cayo Largo lies to the south of Cuba, a half-hour flight from Havana. Four hotels are at the disposal of tourists. Don't expect too much of the food and lodgings, but the beaches! Glistening white sand borders the roughly twenty-mile-long island with its gentle bays. Beaches backed by palm groves and cliffs and with names that sound like music: Playa Blanca, Playa los Cocos, Playa Tortuga, Playa Luna. And the most wonderful part is that once you get away from the hotel beaches, you can find bays of dreamlike beauty and simply claim them for yourself and your lover.

CUBA'S CARNIVAL, RESURRECTED AFTER
A LONG FORCED PAUSE, IS NEITHER SO
SPLENDID NOR SO AMBITIOUS AS RIO'S.
NEVERTHELESS IT POSSESSES AN EXPRESSIVE
ENERGY HARD FOR AN OUTSIDER TO
FATHOM, A SENSUAL EXCITEMENT AND
A CHARM WITH NOTHING COMMERCIAL
ABOUT IT.

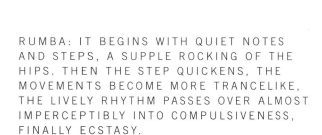

RUMBA: IT BEGINS WITH QUIET NOTES
AND STEPS, A SUPPLE ROCKING OF THE
HIPS. THEN THE STEP QUICKENS, THE
MOVEMENTS BECOME MORE TRANCELIKE,
THE LIVELY RHYTHM PASSES OVER ALMOST
IMPERCEPTIBLY INTO COMPULSIVENESS,
FINALLY ECSTASY.

EVERY CITY HAS ITS OWN SMELL. HAVANA SMELLS OF
TOBACCO, RUM, AND LOVELY GIRLS. OF A LUST FOR LIFE
AND OF MELANCHOLY, OF FORGETTING AND OF HOPE. ITS
PEOPLE KNOW THAT LIFE IS SHORT, AND THEY ENJOY IT.

Acknowledgments

THE SUPPORT GIVEN US IN OUR RESEARCH AND PICTURE TAKING
BOTH IN CUBA AND HERE AT HOME WAS AS UNCOMPLICATED AND
FRIENDLY AS THE CUBANS THEMSELVES.

Sincere thanks to:

• my colleague Rolando Quinones, the bartender at the Floridita in Havana—
to my mind the best and most professional bartender in Cuba (he used to serve
Hemingway)—for his support and insider information about Cuban rum drinks
and their original recipes

• the staff of the Bodeguita del Medio in Havana

Ernst Lechthaler

WE ARE ESPECIALLY GRATEFUL TO THE FOLLOWING
INSTITUTIONS, BUSINESSES, AND INDIVIDUALS:

• the Cuban tourist office in Frankfurt for taking care of us in Cuba

• IGM, Koblenz, sole German importer of Havana Club, the genuine rum from Cuba

• Heinrich Villiger and his 5th Avenue Products Trading, the exclusive importer
into Germany of Havana cigars

• Sylvia Mendez, our translator in Cuba

• Massimo Bassano for photographic assistance

LEFT: ERNST LECHTHALER WITH GREGORIO FUENTES (BORN 1901), SKIPPER AND CLOSE FRIEND OF HEMINGWAY, CAPTAIN OF HIS BOAT THE *PILAR*, AND THE MODEL FOR THE TITLE CHARACTER IN *THE OLD MAN AND THE SEA*.

RIGHT: ERNST LECHTHALER WITH FIDEL CASTRO.

ABOUT THE AUTHORS

ERNST LECHTHALER is one of Munich's most inventive bartenders and is a frequent visitor to Cuba. He is the author of several books and magazine articles on catering and bartending.

AUGUST F. WINKLER writes about drinks and cigars in magazines and newspapers.

ABOUT THE PHOTOGRAPHER

AMIEL PRETSCH lives in Milan and Munich. He is a well-known photographer and producer of print ads and television commercials for such clients as Swatch and BMW.

Index of Drinks